Country Breakfasts

■ · ■ · ■ · ■ · ■ · ■ · ■ · ■ · ■ · ■ · ■

Start Your Day the Old Fashioned Way

Kelsey Dollar

The American Pantry Collection™

Published by:
Apricot Press
Box 1611
American Fork, Utah
84003

books@apricotpress.com
www.apricotpress.com

ISBN 1-885027-31-1

Cover Design & Layout by David Mecham
Printed in the United States of America

This book is dedicated to my grandmother, Carolyn Duncan Allred. Thanks "Grandma C" for all your help and inspiration.

Many thanks to Robyn Allred, Laura Dollar, JoLyn Farrer, Vikki Gillman, Grandma C, and Grandma Drew for their contributions to this book.

Foreword

Breakfast is the most important meal of the day, it also happens to be my favorite. Don't get me wrong, I love lunch and dinner, and a snack here and there is nice too, but in my opinion it doesn't get any better than eggs and bacon, a giant waffle with strawberry jam, or a huge omelet.

As a child, I remember after a sleep-over at grandmas, I could count on having a big breakfast. I would wake to the smell of something extraordinary coming from Grandma's kitchen. I would hurry out to the kitchen and find Grandma, in one of her kitchen aprons, busy around the stove, preparing all sorts of yummy things. Sometimes it was pancakes, crepes or waffles. Other times hot cereal with thick slices of bread and jam. My favorite was poached eggs, bacon, sausage and toast. I also have sweet memories of Saturday morning breakfasts. Mom and Dad would lay out a tasty meal, gather all the kids around the table and we would enjoy a traditional breakfast feast.

Now that I am married, my husband and I have tried to preserve the tradition of family breakfasts; his family also has "Grandpa Dollar Breakfasts."

Each recipe in this book was hand picked especially for you. I am fortunate to have some extraordinary cooks in my family that prepare some of the most scrumptious meals you have ever tasted, and many of these recipes are their brilliant creations. It was difficult to just pick a few favorites because there are so many to choose from. I have also included a few of my own inspirations. The bulk of these recipes are old family favorites, traditions in my family for years. I hope they can bring you just as many satisfied people and full tummies.

To add a bit of character and charm, I have used a few quotations and sayings from Benjamin Franklin's Poor Richard's Almanac. One of my favorites, and I think very wise advice, is, "Early to bed and early to rise, makes a man healthy, wealthy and wise."

- Kelsey Dollar

Contents

Recipes

Baked Apple Oatmeal

2 tablespoons butter
2 cups chopped apples
4 cups boiling water
2 cups raisins
2 cups nuts
4 cups old fashioned oats
2-2/3 cups nonfat dry milk
3/4 cup brown sugar
1 tablespoon salt
2 tablespoons cinnamon

Combine all ingredients and place in 9x13 casserole dish. Bake uncovered at 350° for 30 to 35 minutes.

"Every recipe has a story, even if you don't know the story behind it, it is there just the same. The taste and smell of something can evoke sweet memories of days past. My aunt, who is known as one of the best cooks in the Columbia Basin, gave me this recipe. It has been one of her family's favorites for years."

Biscuits

■ • ■ • ■ • ■ • ■ • ■ • ■ • ■ • ■ • ■ • ■

2 cups sifted flour
1 teaspoon salt
2-1/2 teaspoons baking powder
1/3 cup shortening
2/3 cup milk

Preheat oven to 425°. Combine flour, salt and baking
powder. Using a pastry blender, cut in shortening until
it has the consistency of coarse cornmeal. Add the milk
and toss gently with a two-pronged fork until all
particles are moistened. Gather the dough into a ball
and turn it onto a lightly floured board. Knead the
dough gently about 12 times with the heel of your hand.
Gather into a ball once more. Lightly flour the board
again and roll the dough out with a floured rolling pin to
1/2 inch thickness. Cut dough into rounds with a
floured biscuit cutter. Place on cookie sheet about 1/2
inch apart. Bake at 425° for 12-15 minutes.

■ • ■ • ■ • ■ • ■ • ■ • ■ • ■ • ■ • ■ • ■

Grape Jelly

3-1/2 cups grape juice
1 package M.C.P. Pectin
4-1/2 cups sugar
1/4 cup lemon juice

In a large kettle, combine grape juice and pectin and stir well. Over high heat, bring to a boil, stir constantly to avoid scorching. Add sugar and stir until dissolved. Bring to a boil and boil for exactly 2 minutes. Remove kettle from heat and skim foam off the top. Pour juice into bottles and seal.

"The busy man has few idle visitors; to the boiling pot the flies come not."

"He that has a trade has an estate."

"A good example is the best sermon."

Lead Pancakes

□ · □ · □ · □ · □ · □ · □ · □ · □ · □ · □

3/4 cup flour
1/2 cup rolled oats
1 tablespoon sugar
1 teaspoon baking powder
1/2 teaspoon baking soda
1/2 teaspoon salt
2 tablespoons oil
1 cup buttermilk
1 egg

Beat egg then add remaining ingredients and continue beating until smooth. Cook on a medium hot griddle. Pancakes are usually thick so be sure the middle is cooked.

□ · □ · □ · □ · □ · □ · □ · □ · □ · □ · □

Breakfast Fruit Casserole

▫ • ▫ • ▫ • ▫ • ▫ • ▫ • ▫ • ▫ • ▫ • ▫ • ▫

**1 lemon
1 orange
3 tablespoons brown sugar
1 16-ounce can apricots
1 16-ounce can pineapple chunks
1 16-ounce can sliced peaches
1 16-ounce can pitted cherries
Nutmeg**

Preheat oven to 350°. Drain all canned fruit. Grate lemon and orange rinds and combine with brown sugar. Slice lemon and orange into rings and layer with canned fruit. Sprinkle each layer with brown sugar mixture and nutmeg. Bake for 30 minutes.

Top with sour cream and macaroons or Honey Dressing and lemon rind sprinkles.

▫ • ▫ • ▫ • ▫ • ▫ • ▫ • ▫ • ▫ • ▫ • ▫ • ▫

Honey Dressing

■ • ▫ • ▫ • ▫ • ▫ • ▫ • ▫ • ▫ • ▫ • ▫

2 eggs
1/4 cup lemon juice
2 tablespoons frozen orange juice concentrate
2 tablespoons honey
1/8 teaspoon salt
1/2 cup heavy cream
2 tablespoons grated lemon rind

Whip cream. Beat eggs, add lemon juice, orange juice, honey and salt and cook in a saucepan. Stirring frequently, cook over low heat until dressing thickens. Cool and fold into whipped cream.

■ • ▫ • ▫ • ▫ • ▫ • ▫ • ▫ • ▫ • ▫ • ▫

"When the well is dry—they know the worth of water."

"Early to bed and early to rise, makes a man healthy wealthy and wise."

"Trust thyself and another shall not betray thee."

"Wealth is not his that has it, but his that enjoys it."

Maple Cinnamon Oatmeal

Oatmeal cereal
Cinnamon
Maple syrup

Cook oatmeal according to instructions on the package. Add cinnamon and syrup to taste, add a little to make it light, or more for a sweeter taste.

> *"I like to use quick oats because they are so much easier. I do one part oats to two parts water and boil for about a minute and a half.*

Apple Raisin Muffins

■ • ■ • ■ • ■ • ■ • ■ • ■ • ■ • ■ • ■ • ■

1 cup whole wheat flour (or grain mix flour)
1 cup quick rolled oats
1 tablespoon baking powder
1/2 teaspoon baking soda
1/2 teaspoon salt
1 teaspoon cinnamon
1/4 cup honey or sugar
1 cup milk
1 egg
2 tablespoons oil
1 apple
1/3 cup raisins

Preheat oven to 400°. Grease muffin tins or line with baking cups. Wash and core the apple and cut it into quarters. Mix all dry ingredients. In a blender, combine apple chunks, raisins, milk, egg and oil and blend until finely chopped. Combine wet and dry ingredients and stir until well mixed. Fill baking cups 3/4 full. Bake for 12 to 14 minutes.

■ • ■ • ■ • ■ • ■ • ■ • ■ • ■ • ■ • ■ • ■

Hot Milk Toast

1 tablespoon butter
1 cup milk
2 eggs
salt & pepper
1 slice of toast

Heat butter and milk in a small saucepan. Add eggs and season with salt and pepper. Simmer over low heat until white of eggs are set. Butter toast if desired then cut from corner to corner and place in serving bowl. Spoon eggs from hot milk and place on toast. Pour milk over eggs.

"My great grandpa said this was medicine if you weren't feeling well."

Buttermilk Syrup

■ · ▢ · ▢ · ▢ · ▢ · ▢ · ▢ · ▢ · ▢ · ▢ · ■

2 cups sugar
1 cup buttermilk
1/2 cup butter
2 teaspoons light corn syrup
1 teaspoon baking soda
2 teaspoons vanilla

Combine all ingredients in a deep pan and bring to a boil over medium heat. Boil for 5 minutes, stirring often. Serve over pancakes, waffles or ice cream.

■ · ▢ · ▢ · ▢ · ▢ · ▢ · ▢ · ▢ · ▢ · ▢ · ■

4-Generation Hotcakes

2 cups flour
1 teaspoon baking soda
2 teaspoons baking powder
2 tablespoons sugar
1/4 teaspoon salt
2 cups buttermilk
2 tablespoons oil
2 egg whites, stiffly beaten

Sift dry ingredients together. Gently stir in buttermilk and oil, then fold in egg whites. Don't over mix. Cook on ungreased griddle until browned on both sides.

Tea Time Rolls

■ • ▢ • ▢ • ▢ • ▢ • ▢ • ▢ • ▢ • ▢ • ▢ • ▢

1 tablespoon dry yeast
1-1/4 cups warm water
1/4 cup sugar
1/3 cup nonfat dry milk
1 teaspoon salt
1/3 cup oil
1 egg, beaten
2-1/2 to 3 cups flour

Preheat oven to 375°. Pour warm water into large bowl and sprinkle yeast into water. Add remaining ingredients; batter should be thick, add more flour if needed. Cover and let rise until doubled in size. Stir down and drop spoonfuls onto greased baking pans. Let rise again until doubled. Bake 20 to 30 minutes, until golden brown.

Try topping dough balls with slices of fresh fruit like peaches, plums or apricots. Then combine 1/4 cup butter, 1/4 cup flour, 1/4 cup sugar and 1 teaspoon cinnamon and sprinkle on top of fruit. Let rise and then bake.

■ • ▢ • ▢ • ▢ • ▢ • ▢ • ▢ • ▢ • ▢ • ▢ • ▢

Sunday Breakfast Cake

Cake:
3/4 cup sugar
1 egg
1-1/2 cups flour
1/2 teaspoon salt
1/4 cup butter
1/2 cup milk
2 teaspoons baking powder
   Filling:
1/2 cup brown sugar
2 tablespoons margarine
2 tablespoons flour
1-2 teaspoons cinnamon

Preheat oven to 350°. Butter cake pan. Mix together all ingredients for cake. In a separate bowl, mix all ingredients for filling and layer in cake pan. Bake for 30 minutes.

"Glass, china and reputation are easily cracked and never well mended."

"Work while it is called today for you know not how much you may be hindered tomorrow."

"Plough deep while sluggards sleep and you shall have corn to sell and to keep."

Apple Waffles

2 cups whole wheat flour
1/2 teaspoon salt
1 tablespoon sugar
1 tablespoon baking powder
1/2 teaspoon cinnamon
1/2 teaspoon nutmeg
1/4 teaspoon cloves
2/3 cups dry milk
2 eggs
1/3 cup salad oil
1 teaspoon vanilla
1 apple, cored, peeled and chopped
1-3/4 cups apple juice

Preheat waffle iron. Combine, flour, salt, sugar, baking powder, cinnamon, nutmeg and cloves. In a blender, combine remaining ingredients and blend until mixture is pureed. Combine puree and dry ingredients and mix well. Cook in waffle iron until browned.

Cloud Biscuits

■ • ■ • ■ • ■ • ■ • ■ • ■ • ■ • ■ • ■ • ■

2 cups flour
1 tablespoon sugar
4 teaspoons baking powder
1/2 teaspoon salt
1/2 cup shortening or margarine
1 beaten egg
2/3 cup milk

Preheat oven to 450°. Sift together flour, salt, sugar and baking powder. Cut in shortening until coarsely mixed. Combine milk and egg, then add to flour mixture. Turn onto lightly floured board and roll until 3/4 inch thick. Cut into biscuits and place on greased cookie sheet. Chill 1 to 3 hours (optional). Bake for 10 to 14 minutes.

■ • ■ • ■ • ■ • ■ • ■ • ■ • ■ • ■ • ■ • ■

"Want of care does us more damage than want of knowledge."

"Each year one vicious habit rooted out, in time might make the worst man good throughout."

"Tis hard but glorious to be poor and honest."

Best Omelet

2 tablespoons Minute Tapioca
3/4 teaspoon salt
1/8 teaspoon pepper
3/4 cup milk
1 tablespoon butter
4 eggs

Butter and preheat frying pan, also preheat oven to 350°.
Combine tapioca, salt and pepper in a saucepan; stir and
add milk. Over medium heat, stir and cook until
mixture comes to a full boil. Mix in butter and remove
from heat. Allow to cool slightly. In a separate bowl,
beat egg whites until stiff. In another bowl, beat egg
yolks until thick. Blend tapioca mixture gradually into
egg yolks then fold in egg whites. Pour into frying pan
and cook over low heat for about 3 minutes. Place
frying pan in oven and bake for 15 minutes. Omelet is
done when knife inserted into the middle comes out
clean.

Serve with salsa.

"Omelets are a wonderful creation; each one is unique and the possibilities are endless. Omelets can be customized to any taste. A basic omelet begins with three eggs, then add whatever suits your fancy to make the omelet yours. Anything can be added, cheese, any kind of meat, any vegetable, basically anything you can find. Some people like their omelets more like a scramble, others prefer all the fixings to be wrapped inside an outer layer of egg, almost like a burrito. No matter what your taste buds are craving, you can likely satisfy them with an omelet."

Breakfast Burrito

■ • ■ • ■ • ■ • ■ • ■ • ■ • ■ • ■ • ■

8 eggs
2/3 cup milk
1-1/2 teaspoon salt
1/2 teaspoon pepper
1-1/2 cup shredded cheese
2/3 cup meat of your choice, chopped
1/2 cup chopped tomatoes
1/4 cup chopped onions
1/4 cup chopped bell peppers
4 flour tortillas

Saute onions and peppers until tender. Whip eggs, milk, salt, pepper and cheese. Remove onions and peppers from frying pan; pour egg mixture into pan and cook and stir until almost firm. Add meat and vegetables and blend into eggs. Roll egg mixture into tortilla and serve with salsa or sour cream.

■ • ■ • ■ • ■ • ■ • ■ • ■ • ■ • ■ • ■

Green Chile Sauce (Chile Verde)

■ ・ ■ ・ ■ ・ ■ ・ ■ ・ ■ ・ ■ ・ ■ ・ ■ ・ ■ ・ ■

1 tablespoon shortening
1 cup chicken broth
   or 2 cups tomatoes with liquid
1/2 cup chopped onion
1/4 teaspoon garlic salt
2 tablespoons flour
3/4 teaspoon salt
1 cup chopped green chilies
   (more or less can be used according to your taste)

Heat shortening in a medium-size skillet on medium heat and saute' chopped onion. Add flour and cook for one minute. Add all remaining ingredients and simmer for 20 minutes.

■ ・ ■ ・ ■ ・ ■ ・ ■ ・ ■ ・ ■ ・ ■ ・ ■ ・ ■ ・ ■

Tomato Pancakes

■ • ■ • ■ • ■ • ■ • ■ • ■ • ■ • ■ • ■ • ■

4 eggs, beaten
1 can stewed or diced tomatoes with liquid
2 cups home-canned tomatoes
40 single soda crackers
   (about 4 ounces - hand crushed - not rolled out)
salt to taste
butter for frying

Mix together beaten eggs, tomatoes, crackers and salt.
Shape into 4-inch pancakes and fry over medium heat in
a small amount of butter, 2 minutes on each side.

■ • ■ • ■ • ■ • ■ • ■ • ■ • ■ • ■ • ■ • ■

"Beware of little expenses, a small leak will sink a great ship."

"The proud have pride—in others."

"At the working man's house hunger looks in but dares not enter."

Dripper Breakfast

3 cups cubed French bread
1 cup grated cheese
1/2 cup chopped onion
1/2 cup chopped green pepper
1 can mushrooms, drained
1/2 cup chopped tomatoes
10 eggs, beaten
4 cups milk
1 teaspoon prepared mustard
1 teaspoon salt
1/4 teaspoon onion powder
1/4 teaspoon pepper
10 slices of cooked bacon

Arrange bread in bottom of a buttered 9x13 baking pan. Layer with cheese, onion, green pepper, mushrooms and tomatoes. In a separate bowl combine beaten eggs, milk, mustard, salt, onion powder and pepper. Mix and pour over layers. Crumble bacon slices over the top. Bake at 325° for 1 hour and 15 minutes.

Grandma's Famous Pancakes

2 eggs
2 cups milk
1 tablespoon sugar
1/4 teaspoon salt
3 tablespoons butter or shortening
2 cups flour
5 teaspoons baking powder

Combine eggs, milk and sugar, beat well. Then add salt,
butter, flour and baking powder. Beat well and pour
onto lightly greased griddle and fry until golden brown.

German Pancakes

6 eggs
1 cup flour
1 cup milk
1/2 teaspoon salt
butter

Melt some butter in a 9 x 13 pan. Mix all ingredients well in blender and pour into pan. Bake at 425° for 25 minutes.

"Serve with butter and syrup or jam and whipped cream."

"Shortly after I was married, my husband and I were trying to decide what to make for breakfast one Saturday morning. He asked me if he could make "Creepy Crawlers." I had no idea what dish he was referring to, and was disgusted at the thought of eating something that was creepy or crawly and quickly said I didn't think that sounded very appetizing. He protested by pointing out that he loved them and my mom and grandmother make them all the time and that I never complain when they make them so why didn't I want them today?"

"I finally figured out that his mom also makes what I know as German Pancakes. My husband called them Creepy Crawlers because of the way they move when they are in the oven. We both enjoyed our Creepy Crawly German Pancakes that morning."

"Well done, is twice done."

"Think of three things: Whence you came, Where you are going, and to whom you must account."

"Having been poor is no shame; but being ashamed of it is."

Homemade Syrup

2 cups sugar
1 cup corn syrup
2 cups water
1 teaspoon maple flavoring

Mix all ingredients in pan and bring to a boil. Serve hot or cold.

Golden Rod

4 hard boiled eggs
1/4 cup butter
3 tablespoons flour
1/4 teaspoon salt
1/8 teaspoon pepper
2-1/2 cups milk
1/2 loaf of bread, toasted

Peel eggs and dice the whites. Grate yolks into a separate bowl. In a saucepan, melt butter and stir in flour, salt and pepper. Stirring constantly, slowly add milk. Heat on low until sauce thickens. Stir in chopped egg whites and pour over toast. Sprinkle grated egg yolks on top.

Buttermilk Pancakes

■ · ■ · ■ · ■ · ■ · ■ · ■ · ■ · ■ · ■ · ■

2 cups buttermilk
2 eggs, separated
2 cups flour
2 teaspoons baking powder
1 teaspoon baking soda
1/2 teaspoon salt
1/2 cup melted butter

Combine buttermilk and egg yolks and mix. In a separate bowl, combine dry ingredients. Add dry ingredients to wet and mix well. Add melted butter and stir. Whip egg whites to a stiff peak and fold into batter. Fry on a hot griddle.

"These pancakes make great waffles if you cook in a waffle iron instead of on a griddle."

■ · ■ · ■ · ■ · ■ · ■ · ■ · ■ · ■ · ■ · ■

Finish Crepes (Ohukaisia)

3 large eggs
1 quart milk
2/3 cup sugar
2 cups flour
1/2 teaspoon salt
3 tablespoons melted butter

Combine ingredients and stir until smooth. Add more flour for thicker crepes or less for thinner ones. Fry like pancakes on a griddle. Serve with melted butter and sugar rolled up or folded in half with jam inside and topped with cream.

"This recipe is one of my family favorites. We make it at almost every family gathering."

"Crepes are a tradition in my family for sleepovers, family reunions or parties. My dad is famous for his Finish Crepes (he lived in Finland for two years as a young man) and is often asked to cook them for groups of friends or church parties or family gatherings."

"In Finland, many people eat crepes every day. They serve them every way you can imagine. Dad and his roommate would make a batch of crepes in the morning and eat them warm with melted butter and sugar; then they would roll them up and put them in their sacks and eat them cold at lunchtime."

"When I was growing up, we ate them the Finish way, with butter and sugar, we also love them with jam or preserves topped with whipped cream. Crepes are so versatile you can even make a Breakfast Wrap using eggs and sausage, bacon or ham. Crepes are sure to be one of your favorites!"

"If you were a servant would you not be ashamed that a good master should catch you idle? Then if you are your own master be ashamed to catch yourself idle."

"Wink at small faults; remember thou hast great ones."

Helen's Quiche

3/4 cup sliced onion
2 tablespoons butter
9-inch pie shell
8 ounces shredded Swiss and Cheddar cheese
1 cup light cream
3 eggs, beaten
1 tablespoon flour
1/2 teaspoon salt
1/4 teaspoon dry mustard
1/8 teaspoon pepper
1 teaspoon Worcestershire sauce
1 cup cubed ham

Preheat oven to 350°. Sauté onion in butter until tender, do not brown. Spread in bottom of unbaked pie shell. Top with cheese. Combine cream and eggs and mix. In a separate bowl, combine flour, salt, mustard and pepper, mix and add to milk mixture. Add Worcestershire sauce. Pour mixture over onions and cheese in pie shell. Top with ham and bake for 50 minutes to 1 hour.

Breakfast Casserole

4 slices bread
1 cup grated cheddar cheese
1 pound link sausages
1 dozen eggs
1/2 green bell pepper, chopped
3 green onions, chopped with tops
1-1/2 cups milk
3/4 teaspoon dry mustard
salt and pepper
1 can cream of mushroom soup
1/2 cup milk

Cut bread into strips. Dice sausage if desired, then cook and drain it. Line greased 9x13 baking pan with bread strips. Sprinkle with cheese and sausage links. In a separate bowl, combine eggs, peppers, onion, 1-1/2 cups milk, mustard, salt and pepper and mix well. Pour over bread and refrigerate over night.

Preheat oven to 300°. Mix soup and 1/2 cup milk and pour over the top. Bake uncovered for 90 minutes.

Swedish Pancakes

3/4 cup sifted flour
2 eggs, beaten
1 cup milk
1/2 teaspoon salt
1 tablespoon oil
1 tablespoon sugar

Combine dry ingredients. In a separate bowl, beat eggs then add milk and oil. Pour into dry ingredients and beat until smooth. Cook on hot griddle 1 tablespoon at a time, cakes will be very thin.

"Take this remark from Richard poor and lame, Whatever is begun in anger ends in shame."

"Blessed is he who expects nothing, for he shall never be disappointed."

"Have you something to do tomorrow? Do it today."

"If you would reap praise you must sow the seeds, gentle words and useful deeds."

Belgian Waffles

3 egg yolks
1 cup milk
1/2 cup melted butter
1 tablespoon vanilla
2 cups flour
1/2 teaspoon salt
1 tablespoon baking powder
1/4 cup sugar

Mix egg yolks, milk, butter and vanilla. Combine dry ingredients. Add dry to wet and mix well. In a separate bowl, whisk egg whites until soft peaks form. Fold egg whites into mixture and cook in waffle iron. Top with fresh berries and whipped cream.

Fruit Syrup

■ · ■ · ■ · ■ · ■ · ■ · ■ · ■ · ■ · ■ · ■

6 ounces frozen juice concentrate
   (cherry, berry or peach are my favorites)
6 ounces water
1/2 tablespoon cornstarch

Dissolve cornstarch in water. Whisk mixture into
thawed juice concentrate. Stirring constantly, heat over
medium heat until boiling. Serve warm or cold over
pancakes, waffles, or French toast.

■ · ■ · ■ · ■ · ■ · ■ · ■ · ■ · ■ · ■ · ■

Chocolate Crepes

■ · ▢ · ▢ · ▢ · ▢ · ▢ · ▢ · ▢ · ▢ · ▢ · ▢

2 cups milk
2 eggs
3 tablespoons melted butter
1-1/2 cups flour
1/3 cup cocoa powder
1/2 cup sugar
1/2 teaspoon salt

In a blender, combine milk, eggs, butter, flour, cocoa, sugar and salt. Blend until batter is smooth. Fry on a hot griddle like pancakes. Serve hot with jam and whipped cream.

■ · ▢ · ▢ · ▢ · ▢ · ▢ · ▢ · ▢ · ▢ · ▢ · ▢

Scones

2 cups scalded milk
1/2 cup shortening
3 tablespoons yeast
1/2 cup very warm water
1/2 cup sugar
3 eggs, beaten
1 teaspoon salt
6-7 cups flour

Add yeast to warm water, stir until dissolved, then add sugar. Combine all remaining ingredients and add yeast mixture. Mix well; roll out on floured board. Cut into squares. Fry squares in hot oil. Serve warm with jam or honey butter.

Honey Butter

1/2 cup butter
1/2 cup honey
1/4 teaspoon vanilla

Whip softened butter. Add vanilla and gradually add honey while whipping.

"Dost thou love life? Then do not squander time; for that's the stuff life is made of."

"Most people return small favors, acknowledge middling ones, and repay great ones with ingratitude."

Potato Pancakes

■ • ■ • ■ • ■ • ■ • ■ • ■ • ■ • ■ • ■ • ■

4 medium potatoes
1 minced onion
2 tablespoons flour
1/8 teaspoon nutmeg
1 egg, slightly beaten
1/2 teaspoon salt
butter for frying

Peel and grate potatoes. Combine onion, flour, nutmeg, egg, salt and mix. Add to potatoes. Place mounds of potato dough in melted butter in a heavy frying pan. Flatten with pancake turner. Fry approximately 5 minutes. Top with apple sauce and sour cream.

■ • ■ • ■ • ■ • ■ • ■ • ■ • ■ • ■ • ■ • ■

Bread and Milk

Slices of bread
Milk or heavy cream

Break up slices of bread into a bowl. Pour milk over the top. If desired, add jam, jelly or honey for a sweet treat. Or try cheese slices and green onions.

"This was one of my grandparents' favorite breakfasts and snacks. My dad and grandpa still enjoy their bread and milk after a long day."

Blintzes

2 large eggs
1 cup cottage cheese
1/3 cup milk
1/4 cup flour
1 teaspoon vanilla

Beat egg whites until stiff. In a blender, combine
cottage cheese and egg yolks and blend until smooth.
Add milk, flour and vanilla and blend well. Pour into a
separate bowl then fold in egg whites. Fry on a greased,
hot griddle. Turn when top is bubbly. Both sides
should be browned. Serve with jam and whipped cream
or syrup.

"The noblest question in the world is,
What good may I do in it?"

"What you would seem to be, be really."

"Tricks and treachery are the practice of
fools that have not wit enough to be
honest."

Apple Butter

4 cups water
10 cups sugar
1/2 bushel tart apples
2 teaspoon cloves
2 tablespoon cinnamon
1 teaspoon allspice

Wash apples and quarter them, leave unpeeled. In a large pan, cook in water; let simmer slowly until apples are tender. Put through coarse sieve. This makes about 5 quarts of apple pulp. Add 1 part sugar to 2 parts pulp, then add spices. Simmer again for 2 hours, apple butter scorches easily, so stir it frequently. When butter is thickened, pour into jars and seal. As it cools it becomes stiffer.

Skier's French Toast

2 tablespoon corn syrup
1/2 cup butter
1 cup brown sugar, packed
5 eggs
1-1/2 teaspoon vanilla
1/3 teaspoon salt
1 loaf of bread

In a saucepan, combine corn syrup, margarine and brown sugar; simmer until syrupy. Pour syrup into a 9x13 casserole dish. Place 12 to 16 slices of bread over syrup mixture. In a separate bowl, beat together eggs, milk, vanilla and salt. Pour over bread. Cover and refrigerate overnight. Preheat oven to 350°. Bake uncovered for 45 minutes. Serve warm. Can be reheated later.

Biscuits and Gravy

■ · ■ · ■ · ■ · ■ · ■ · ■ · ■ · ■ · ■ · ■

Biscuits
1/2 pound sausage
1 cup milk
2 rounded tablespoons flour
salt & pepper

Crumble sausage in frying pan and brown and drain. In a separate bowl, mix milk, flour and salt and pepper. Add to sausage and cook on medium-high heat until desired thickness. Cut biscuits in half and cover with gravy.

■ · ■ · ■ · ■ · ■ · ■ · ■ · ■ · ■ · ■ · ■

"He that composes himself is wiser than he that composes books."

"Fear to do evil and you need fear nothing else."

Whole Wheat Pancakes

1 cup milk
1 cup whole kernel wheat
2 to 3 eggs
1 tablespoon sugar or honey
1/4 teaspoon salt
4 tablespoons oil
1 teaspoon baking soda
2 teaspoons baking powder

In a blender, blend milk and wheat. Liquify for 4 minutes. While blender is still going add remaining ingredients, adding baking powder last. Blend until all ingredients are mixed together. Let rest for 10 to 15 minutes. Cook on hot oiled griddle.

Deluxe Hot Cakes

■ · ■ · ■ · ■ · ■ · ■ · ■ · ■ · ■ · ■ · ■

1-1/2 cup sifted flour
1 teaspoon baking powder
3/4 teaspoon salt
3 tablespoons sugar*
2 egg yolks
1-1/2 cups whole milk
3 tablespoons oil
2 egg whites, beaten

Combine in this order: flour, baking powder, salt, sugar, egg yolks, milk and oil, then fold in egg whites. Lightly grease hot griddle and cook until browned. My favorite way to serve these pancakes is with creamy peanut better and maybe a little maple syrup

* This hot cake recipe is sweeter than normal. Reduce sugar if desired.

■ · ■ · ■ · ■ · ■ · ■ · ■ · ■ · ■ · ■ · ■

Breakfast Quiche

■ · ▣ · ▣ · ▣ · ▣ · ▣ · ▣ · ▣ · ▣ · ▣ · ▣

1/2 cup biscuit mix
3 eggs
2 cups milk
1/2 teaspoon salt
Cayenne pepper (to taste)
1/2 teaspoon prepared mustard
8 slices crispy bacon, crumbled
1 cup shredded cheese (Cheddar or Swiss)

Preheat oven to 350°. Grease 8 or 9 inch pie pan. In a
blender, combine biscuit mix, eggs, milk, salt, pepper
and mustard. Blend for 2 minutes. Pour into pie pan.
Sprinkle bacon and cheese on top, press cheese down.
Bake 30 to 40 minutes, quiche is done when it is set.

■ · ▣ · ▣ · ▣ · ▣ · ▣ · ▣ · ▣ · ▣ · ▣ · ▣

"A slip of the foot you may soon recover;
But a slip of the tongue you may never
get over."

"One today is worth two tomorrows."

"Wish not so much to live long as to
live well."

Breakfast Tarts

■ · □ · □ · □ · □ · □ · □ · □ · □ · □ · □

1/2 pound pork sausage
1/4 cup melted butter
2 tablespoons boiling water
1-1/4 cups biscuit mix
1 egg, slightly beaten
1/2 cup half and half
2 tablespoons scallions, chopped
1/2 cup shredded cheese
   (Cheddar, Mozzarella or Swiss)

Preheat oven to 375°. Grease and flour muffin tins.
Crumble and brown sausage. Combine biscuit mix,
butter and water and mix well. In a separate bowl,
combine egg, half and half and scallions and mix well.
Press 1 tablespoon biscuit dough into bottom and sides
of muffin tins, spoon meat evenly on top of dough.
Place 2 tablespoons of egg mixture into each muffin cup.
Bake for 20 minutes then sprinkle cheese over the top of
muffin cups and bake 5 more minutes.

■ · □ · □ · □ · □ · □ · □ · □ · □ · □ · □

Brunch Egg Bake

3 cups shredded Cheddar cheese
3 cups shredded Mozzarella cheese
1 can mushroom pieces
1/3 cup sliced green onions
1/2 cup chopped bell pepper
2 tablespoons butter
8 eggs
1/2 cup flour
1/4 teaspoon pepper
2 cups diced ham
1-3/4 cups milk
1/2 teaspoon salt

Preheat oven to 350°. Combine cheese and place 1 cup of mixed cheese in ungreased 13x9 baking dish. Saute mushrooms, onions and bell pepper in butter; spread over cheese and top with ham. Sprinkle remaining cheese on top. Beat eggs, then add milk, flour, salt and pepper and mix well. Slowly pour over cheese. Bake for 35 to 40 minutes. Allow to cool for 10 minutes before cutting and serving.

"I never saw an oft-transplanted tree, nor yet an oft-removed family, that throve so well as those that settled be."

"Be always ashamed to catch thyself idle."

Fried Eggs and Bacon

1 pound bacon
8 large eggs
salt and pepper

In a large frying pan, fry bacon until crispy, keep in mind that it continues to cook until it has cooled down a bit, even when it has been removed from frying pan. Set bacon aside and pat grease off with a paper towel. Drain excess grease into a tin can (or something else it won't melt) leave just a bit to cook eggs in. Crack eggs in hot bacon grease. Cook for a minute or so on medium high heat for over easy, or five minutes on medium low for well done. Salt and pepper tops of eggs just before you flip them.

"Eggs are the original breakfast food. They have been the centerpiece for breakfast spreads for generations. You can cook eggs however you like them, sunny side up, over easy, medium, well or anywhere in between if you mess up or break the yolk, just make it a scramble or an omelet. My favorite is medium well, then I dip my toast in the yolk. My husband loves over easy, then he makes a sandwich with two slices of bread and smashes it so the yolks pop and drip everywhere.

With eggs, the possibilities are endless, you can stick with what you know, or be creative. I know people that make sandwiches, wraps or put them on top of hashed browns. Top them with cream cheese, ketchup, salsa, cheese, anything for variety."

Sweet Rolls

■ ▪ ■ ▪ ■ ▪ ■ ▪ ■ ▪ ■ ▪ ■ ▪ ■ ▪ ■ ▪ ■

1/2 cup warm water
1-1/2 cups milk
6 cups flour
1/2 cup shortening
1/2 cup raisins
2 yeast cakes
1/2 cup sugar
2 teaspoons salt
2 eggs
1 teaspoon cinnamon or vanilla

Dissolve yeast in water. Sift dry ingredients and add to beaten eggs, shortening and milk. Knead; let raise until light. Roll to 1/2 inch thick. Sprinkle with sugar and cinnamon and raisins. Roll as a jelly roll and cut into 1 inch pieces. Place cut side up in pan. Let raise until doubled in size. Bake at 400° until browned. May be frosted when cool.

■ ▪ ■ ▪ ■ ▪ ■ ▪ ■ ▪ ■ ▪ ■ ▪ ■ ▪ ■ ▪ ■

"Sell not virtue to purchase wealth nor liberty to purchase power."

"Hear no ill of a friend, nor speak any of an enemy."

"Proclaim not all thou knoweth, all thou owest, all thou hast, nor all thou canst."

Boiled Wheat Cereal

■ • ■ • ■ • ■ • ■ • ■ • ■ • ■ • ■ • ■ • ■

2 cups water
1 cup wheat

In a saucepan, heat water to boiling and add wheat.
Boil until it is desired softness (some people like it
mushy, others like it still firm, almost crunchy)
anywhere from fifteen minutes to an hour.

> *"This recipe is a favorite of my dad's. It is full of fiber and has*
> *virtually no fat. By itself, boiled wheat is pretty bland and*
> *boring, but if you are a bit imaginative, you can create a*
> *delicious breakfast cereal. You can serve it with milk and*
> *brown sugar or maple syrup for a sweet hearty treat. Fresh*
> *fruit or preserves are delicious and not quite as sweet."*

■ • ■ • ■ • ■ • ■ • ■ • ■ • ■ • ■ • ■ • ■

Angel Hair Muffins

1/2 cup butter
1 teaspoon salt
1/2 cup sugar
2 cups scalded milk
3 eggs, beaten
2 yeast cakes
1/2 cup warm water
5-1/2 cups flour

Mix well with a spoon. Let rise, mix so it falls down.
Spoon into muffin tins and bake at 350° until golden
brown.

"Be civil to all, serviceable to many, familiar with few, friend to one, enemy to none."

"Fish and visitors stink in three days."

"An open foe may prove a curse but a pretended friend is worse."

Banana Pancakes

■ • ▫ • ▫ • ▫ • ▫ • ▫ • ▫ • ▫ • ▫ • ▫ • ▫

1 banana
1/4 teaspoon nutmeg
basic pancake batter

Make basic pancake batter either from a mix or use one
of our other recipes in this book. Cut banana into pieces
and stir into batter, add nutmeg and mix well. Fry on a
hot griddle. Top with syrup, or yogurt for a yummy
treat.

*"This is a unique variation of a traditional pancake. Anytime
you add fruit to a pancake you're in for a treat; bananas are
just one of the many fruits you can try for a diversion from
original homestyle or buttermilk pancakes. Use your
imagination when you're cooking pancakes, they are very hard
to ruin."*

▫ • ▫ • ▫ • ▫ • ▫ • ▫ • ▫ • ▫ • ▫ • ▫

Apple Nut Bread

■ · ■ · ■ · ■ · ■ · ■ · ■ · ■ · ■ · ■ · ■

3 eggs
1 cup oil
1 cup sugar
1/3 cup molasses
2 teaspoons vanilla
2 cups flour
1/2 cup whole wheat flour
1 teaspoon salt
1 teaspoon baking soda
1/2 teaspoon baking powder
2 teaspoons cinnamon
2 cups shredded apple
1 cup chopped nuts

Preheat oven to 350°. Beat eggs, then add oil, sugar, molasses, and vanilla. Beat until thick and foamy. Combine dry ingredients and add to egg mixture. Stir until just blended. Add apples and nuts and mix well. Divide batter into 2 greased and floured loaf pans. Bake 45 minutes to 1 hour.

■ · ■ · ■ · ■ · ■ · ■ · ■ · ■ · ■ · ■ · ■

"Success has ruined many a man."

"You can bear your own faults, and why not a fault in your wife?"

"A quarrelsome man has no good neighbors."

Pear Sauce (for pancakes and waffles)

3 pear halves
2 tablespoons maple syrup
1/2 teaspoon vanilla

Chop pears into bite sized pieces or smaller, depending on your preference. Add syrup and vanilla. Heat until warm.

Serves one. Multiply measurements for larger amounts.

Carrot Muffins

1-1/3 cups buttermilk
1 tablespoon oil
4 egg whites
3 tablespoons honey
1 cup rolled oats
1/2 cup whole wheat flour
1/2 cup cornmeal
2 teaspoons baking powder
1/4 teaspoon salt
1 teaspoon cinnamon
1 cup shredded carrots

Preheat oven to 400°. Beat together buttermilk, oil, egg whites and honey. Add dry ingredients and mix. Fold in carrots. Fill muffin tins 1/2 full. Bake 15 to 20 minutes.

Dumplings

2 cups flour
2 teaspoons baking powder
1/2 teaspoon salt
1/2 teaspoon cream of tartar
1/3 cup sugar
1/3 cup shortening
1 cup milk
1 egg

Preheat oven to 425°. Combine dry ingredients and mix.
Cut in shortening until coarse. In a separate bowl,
combine egg and milk and blend into dry ingredients.

Fruit Sauce for Dumplings

1 quart bottled cherries
1/2 packet dry Jello (cherry or strawberry)
sugar
nutmeg

Pour cherries into frying pan; there needs to be about 4 cups of juice, if there isn't add extra water. Add jello to thicken. Add extra sugar if you like it sweeter. Simmer fruit, then drop in dumplings by the spoonful and sprinkle with nutmeg. Steam dumplings about15 minutes.

Eggs in a Basket

1 slice of bread
1 egg
Salt & Pepper
Butter

Butter both sides of bread. Cut round circle out of the
middle with a knife, cup or biscuit cutter. Place bread in
a frying pan. Break egg into center of bread. Season
with salt and pepper. When egg and bread is browned,
turn and brown other side. Also brown middle circles of
bread for toast.

'The American Pantry' Cookbooks

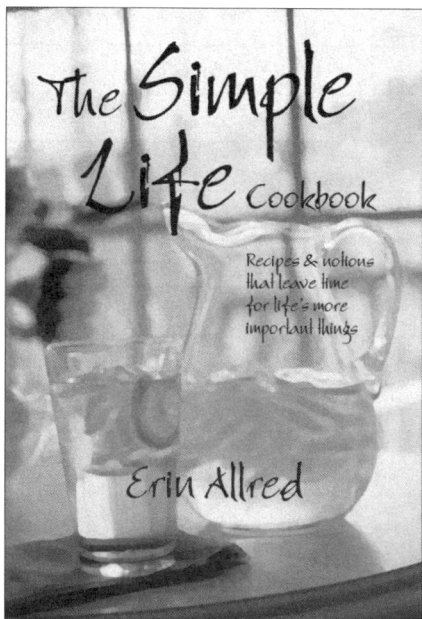

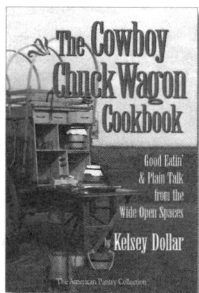

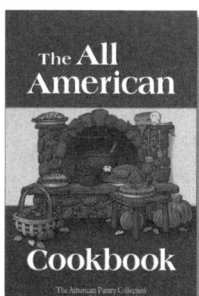

The Simple Life Cookbook

Recipes & notions
that leave time
for life's more
important things

Erin Allred

A Mormon Cookbook

Food, Facts & Friendship
by Erin A. Delfoe
The American Pantry Collection

The Cowboy Chuck Wagon Cookbook

Good Eatin'
& Plain Talk
from the
Wide Open Spaces

Kelsey Dollar
The American Pantry Collection

The Chili & Tomato Cookbook

The American Pantry Collection

Five-Alarm Cooking

"For those who just can't get it hot enough"

Erin Allred
The American Pantry Collection

The All American Cookbook

The American Pantry Collection

All cookbooks are $9.95 US.

Apricot Press Order Form

Book Title	Quantity	x	Cost / Book	=	Total
_____	_____		_____		_____
_____	_____		_____		_____
_____	_____		_____		_____
_____	_____		_____		_____
_____	_____		_____		_____
_____	_____		_____		_____
_____	_____		_____		_____
_____	_____		_____		_____
_____	_____		_____		_____

Do not send Cash. Mail check or money order to:
**Apricot Press   P.O. Box 1611
American Fork, Utah   84003**
Telephone 801-756-0456
Allow 3 weeks for delivery.

**Quantity discounts available.
Call us for more information.**
9 a.m. - 5 p.m. MST

Sub Total =

Shipping = **$2.00**

Tax 8.5% =

Total Amount Enclosed =

Shipping Address

Name:

Street:

City: State:

Zip Code:

Telephone:

Email: